CROSSING OVER

TONY CURTIS
CROSSING OVER

seren

seren is the book imprint of
Poetry Wales Press Ltd.
57 Nolton Street, Bridgend, Wales,CF31 3AE
www.seren-books.com

The right of Tony Curtis to be identified as
the author of this work has been asserted in accordance
with the Copyright, Designs and Patents Act, 1988.

© Copyright Tony Curtis, 2007

ISBN 987-1-85411-437-2

A CIP record for this title is available from the British Library.

The publisher acknowledges the financial assistance of the Welsh Books
Council.

Cover painting : 'The Poet's House' by Charles Burton

Printed in Hoefler by Bell & Bain, Glasgow

Contents

Megan's First Snow	7
From the Book of Hours	8
The Hourglass Tree	9
Midnight Walk	11
Mapping the World	12
Concerning Some Pictures	13
Diving with Mr Jeppers	15
A Noble Going	16
An Order from Mr Kokoschka	17
The Rape of the Sabines	19
La Cathédrale Engloutie	20
Veronese's *Perseus and Andromeda*	21
Le Mangeur De Pommes De Terre	22
A Flemish Landscape	23
Dai Greatcoat Visits Waterloo	24
Morning on the Meuse	26
Dark Night of the Soul	28
Auerbach	29
William Brown's *Circus*	30
Prendergast's Quarry	31
Abandoned Barge – Colin Jones	32
Working the Beech	33
Richard Long's *Buzzard*	34
Moore	35
The Stone Collector	36
Going West	37
Turning	38
At Gumfreston Church	39
The Folly	40
Last Rights	41
Fragile Tissue	42
Barafundle Bay	44
The Plot	46
The Alvis Hare	47
The Trenches At Giltar	48
An Evening Walk to the Sea	49

Yosemite   50
Sirens   51
The Light   52
The Famine Museum   53
The Final Shift   54
John Petts at the Falls   55
Crossing Over   56
Taking Your Food   57
The Morning Round   59
Late Fall   60
Tuscany Postcards for Joan   61
That *Music Lover's Literary Companion*   66
From the Garden   68
Slow Worm   69

Acknowledgements   71

MEGAN'S FIRST SNOW

Snow came floating through the black night,
your side of the channel, our side,
so here this morning
that dusting on our lawn has settled
in the corners of the garden,
crisp and tightening in the sun.

Not enough left now
to make a shroud or a marriage sheet,
but that patch beneath the privet
could be a gentleman's handkerchief.
Yes, I have decided, for us such token white
shall be *a gentleman's handkerchief,*
our code for what remains of snow,
one of the things only you and I know.

FROM THE BOOK OF HOURS

A Nativity, of course,
By the Master of the Circle of Wales,
Provenance – Pembrokeshire, Gwynedd,
And the County of Essex.
Rare: at Sotheby's.

The mother is at the centre,
Her breast its own halo,
That warmth giving the lie to Winter.
The trees are bare, silver and grey
But strong to hold the Spring's growth.

Beyond, through the doorway
A road leads up to the green hill,
The walled edge of a promised city.
The afternoon sky is blue and light
With high clouds touched by gold.

It all comes to this point,
A new beginning.

The border has berries,
Butterflies, song-birds,
And a motif of twining roses,
Red and white.
There are no thorns.

In such a work
An historiated margin might
Well have been anticipated,
While all the prayers and suffrages may be taken
To be on the reverse.

The kings are arriving
Their shoulders hunched, heads bowed,
Offering a superfluity of gifts. Too late –
This daughter's upturned face
Is already alight.

THE HOURGLASS TREE

My second cousin's husband is constructing a tree:
The Hourglass Tree of Hugh Williams,
from the fly-leaves of Bibles and an aunt's memory,
from parish records and trawling the web.

It's three pages of Word
down and across, which I Copy and Save.
One hundred and fifty-two years.
He fits us in, birth date, end date,

each in our box, with lines
from marriage to children
until they become Holland, Jackson
Bersanti, Trow, Aspinall and Shave.

And it all comes from this photograph:
1899 – with patriarch Hugh and Elizabeth
his wife, holding the stiff pose
in that Bangor studio. Their children grow

tired of the hard chairs and the painted backdrops,
the irritable man under his black cloth.
Near the right edge my grandfather Gwilym,
nine or ten, looking like a schoolboy me.

At twenty he watched his brother walk
through the office door
at the L.M.S. wagon works at Earlestown,
and never saw him again.

Hughie went in to be taken on
and left by another door into the world.
Had he run south? Labouring? A shop?
The King's shilling? Never to be seen.

And this is just one story from our tree.
They'd left the slate boats in Bangor
and gone east for their future,
cap in hand to the railway company.

What petty row, forced flesh, slap of tongue
or sting of tear pushed him out
to a rented room, a single swinging light,
fingering at the torn edge of a thin blanket?

Years later, after the war
a stranger came to the end of their road
asking after Ginny and her son.
He wore cap and muffler

though it was summer,
and a hot one.
Then turned back to the corner
and was gone.

MIDNIGHT WALK

The boats wintering in Dickie's of Bangor
call out in a percussive chorus.
Cradled in slings, perched on their stilts,
blocks, oil drums, sleepers,
they are parked in ranks,
huge sour-cream reflections of street lights,
as if a herd of whales had beached
to weigh themselves in air.

From here my family worked the slate boats
crossing the Irish Sea with stacked slivers of Bethesda.
Tonight in the lee of Snowdon
the mid-January wind is icy but dry.
It plays their rigging and they chime
their metal ropes – *Juelle of York, Eryri, Georgina,
Leisure Time, Aberrhod, Mistress Quickly,*
ringing a peal of aluminium against the masts.

Through this valley of hulls the wind is rattling
out of a starless sky. Walk faster whistling
Steely Dan – *the danger on the rocks is surely past.*
For this is Hitchcock's *The Boats* with some night
music by Cage, or a gamelan – you must write it down.
Walk on through, hunched in your heavy coat
and collar up against the music of these dry sirens
as they sing on the edge of the midnight town.

MAPPING THE WORLD

All maps have ourselves at the centre.
This begins with the Mediterranean,
Then the world the Venetians draw
Moves east to the Turk,
South to the Moor
And the Atlantic route to what will become
The Americas.

All of which was known to Nicolas de Nicolay
Whose *Navigatione del Mondo Novo*
At the end of the sixteenth century
Pressing up into the colder, darker north
Had Hibernia, Irlande – Scotia and Anglia
As two islands floating at the edge of things.

And Cambria, Cymru, Wales?
Less trouble now than the Irish or the Scots,
Already gone, swallowed by Anglia.
With flat-faced England left to out-stare
A narrow, starving Ireland
And the Virgin Queen a reprobate maiden-warrior
Beyond heaven's reprieve and true prayer.

Floating on the warm, green soup of the lagoon,
No Doge ever craved and ate
The salty lamb of Ceredigion,
A Towy sewin netted and baked.
How could they have dreamt our red kites
Imperiously paired, soaring over Powys?
Our walls of hard, blue slate,
Eryri's streams like chilled Soave
Poured generously over rocks?

And that slow turn on the Ridgeway road
That presents to you the jewelled sea
And holy in the sun
The island of Caldey.

CONCERNING SOME PICTURES

I am indebted to your Lordship
for the commission in respect of the works
of M. Canal of his Venice
which I will have despatched this week
with the *Venture*, bound for Southampton Water,
in trust of your safe receipt.

There being two works –
some three feet six inches in height
by four feet and one inch –
fine views of the Grand Canal and especially
the square of Saint Mark.
Very like the sketches you have already.
Also the width of the lagoon itself is displayed
to effect in the second work.

And if your Grace could agree to the thirty guineas
to be that for the two times twenty sequeens
and the carriage of said paintings to England,
then I remain,

                    Your humble & obedient servant.

I should add that your Lordship might observe
that M. Canal does not shirk the actual life
of the place and that in the previous work despatched,
to which you expressed something by way of a reservation,
there is, I recall, a number of barges
of trade and employment arranged
in the right foreground of the Rialto view.
Bargemen and the like busy themselves
and cook beneath their canvas shelters.

The light is an afternoon and shews, I think,
the ancient buildings to best effect.

There is even a woman beating carpets
hung from her balcony; note – another holds a rose.
Beneath, in a corner of her building a man,
it would seem, is passing water – though
this is not to the detriment of the work
and is, I trust, barely discernable.
However, I can well appreciate your Lordship's
sensibilities regarding the latter,
and pray that these new works will not offend.

These two at twenty sequeens will prove of worth,
I vouch. The fellow is whimsical
and varies his prices every day.
And he that has a mind
to have any of his work
must not seem to be too fond of it.

My Lord, the light in this city is almost magical
and this painter – *Canaletto* so characterised –
delivers that truth above all others.
Besides, he is in high reputation here
and people will clamber for his pieces whatever.
Thus, I continue to recommend him,
and remain,

Sir, your servant.

DIVING WITH MISTER JEPPERS

Behind all the cutpurses and our diving's
a device tighter than anything,
better than the slack noose at Tyburn:
for them that dips passes the stuff
to them that fences it, or – and here's the laugh –
advertises it abroad that such a purse as this,
or such a scarf as that has been found
and might well be returned
on the payment of a reward.

Which is a neat thing, more perfect and round
than the wheels of the prison-house cart
as the Newgate Ordinary and his Javelin Men
transport their cargo to the monthly hangings.

When Mister Jeppers had his day,
and a fine summer's day too,
I climbed to watch between the nosegays
and finery up on the high platform.
He that was my master in the thieving arts
bore himself like a Turpin or a Wild –
and he ran off the cart into the air
with a "Good day, ladies & gentl'm'!"

A crack we all could hear.

His head flopped like a sleeping dog,
which is better than those that must have relations
rushing to them and swinging from their legs
to quicken and ease their going.

I stayed until all the condemned had swung,
stayed until the Resurrection Men
had collected their wares,
bundled them into sacks for the surgeons.
And I whistled *Meg, Ol' Meg*
as I watched slow clouds like linen
'kerchiefs emptied from an insider pocket,
carried all the way over the river to the city.
And settled my resolve.

A NOBLE GOING

We cut his Lordship
from neck to crotch
and taking the guts from the cage
did lay them out and examine the same.

We could appraise from these
that the Lord was in fine fettle for such an age
and that, other things apart, he should have last
to his three score years and ten.

At the table following – Mrs Steer
having laid cold pheasant, well-hung,
that day's bread
and a jug of ruby claret –
there was talk of his leave-taking,
the first peer to be hanged before the crowd.
And he for nought but the shooting of his steward
accused of design and deceit with others
upon his lord and master
over a coal-mine at Ashby de la Zouch.

A noble driven to it in his own landau,
dressed all in his silver-spun, white wedding suit.
And the biggest crowd of the popular
from the Tower to Tyburn,
given three hours of spectacle.
A noble going indeed, despite
the unseeming dispute between executioner
and assistant over five guineas
given by the lord as his fee.

No hanged man ever had the like
of his silk-lined box.
But, I declare, when they lie at last
on our table and we slice –
a lordly gut's
no more jewelled than a slut's.

AN ORDER FROM MR KOKOSCHKA

Seamstress, I want your finest work,
Your dearest skill. Pay close attention
To the drawings I have sent.
My love must be truly figured from her hair
To the most exquisite feet
As she is in life and my dreams.

The ribcage, the rump, the limbs
To be fashioned in exact proportion.

My sense of touch must take pleasure
At the points where fatty flesh comes to sinew
And firmness. The face must capture
Those looks I see in my dreams.
She shall be a woman of, say, thirty-five
In her moments of pleasure.

For the belly and breast you must use
The finest horsehair –
Rip open a sofa of quality, if you must,
To form those pouches of delight.

Is it still possible to bring the skeleton to me?
At that stage we should take account of our perceptions.

Then, for the peach skin, I think
We should have a rough silk?
Or the finest canvas? Spare nothing.

The photographs you have sent
Capture her vitality, a convincing similitude.
Alma, my dearest love, is being created.

Pray, continue in our work, but keep her secure.
No man must see this creature,
This perfect doll.

I have patience. It must be her exact.
For the skin we shall need powder and wax.

May the mouth be opened?
And are there teeth and a tongue inside?

2

Oscar is quite mad.
He takes her for coffee,
Props her beside him and whispers in her cloth ear.
At the Opera she is in his box
Then goes home in his carriage.
Her underwear, it is said,
He ordered from Vienna,
A fox fur from Berlin.

3

We were all invited to his garden party
Where the champagne flowed
And the chamber orchestra from the Opera
Played under the stars.
The doll of Mrs Mahler made an entrance,
But soon was passed from guest to drunken guest.
The next morning the postman
Ran away screaming murder –
A headless corpse in Kokoschka's garden!
And the police came, and simply laughed.
The dustmen took it away, I gather,
Later that day, or the next.

THE RAPE OF THE SABINES

Ceri Richards, 1948

That wild dance across the pink land
is a welter of bodies coming out of left field,
a fling of a rape in a hot country where
the legs and the finery of the Sabine women are a blur,
their over-the-shoulder faces determined on flight.
They yield only in their own country.
Except there is one already caught
in a forced, awkward embrace, her head
thrown back so that her hair touches the ground,
her breasts the fruit of all labour.
Her young, un-bearded Roman looks away –
beyond the flurry of the others,
away to the wide, hot land they must people.
They are already one and the same future.

LA CATHEDRALE ENGLOUTIE

i.m. Ceri Richards

The drowned bells keen for the sinner and the knave.
Between felled pillars and glass the damned swim free –
Light and music still play beneath the waves.

The ocean breathes and gulps through caves
So rowdy gulls rise to slice the sky. They flee
The drowned bells, keen for sinners and knaves.

For the dry world above is ruled by power-slaves
Who are deaf to truths, can't see
Light and music still play beneath the waves

That circle and define the land. We must learn to love
And live by old rhythms, each fold of the sea.
The drowned bells keen for the sinners and the knaves

As death claims the weak, the noble and the brave
In equal part. Time's indifferent to sacrifice or plea.
Light and music still play beneath the waves –

Our vision and need, what each soul craves,
Is figured in our fallen churches, as Debussy knew, and Ceri.
The drowned bells keen for the sinners and the knaves,
Light and music still play beneath the waves.

VERONESE'S *PERSEUS AND ANDROMEDA*

Voluptuous Andromeda chained at arm and ankle
To the rock, her scarlet robe akimbo,
Was always going to be saved
And hasn't broken sweat.
Her alarm's balletic.

For now out of a louring sky
Fleet, wing-footed Perseus
Descends to slay Poseidon's sea-dragon
With a stylish backhand
Slash of his blade.

Her sacrifice was to bring peace to the kingdom
Though all is redeemed by a single blow –
Honour saved, peace restored. Thus the world is righted
In spite of the skulking gods. And,
Of course, Perseus wins the maiden's hand.

LE MANGEUR DE POMMES DE TERRE

Constant Permeke

sits in a landscape of potatoes –
earth-brown, shit-brown
where even the golden landscape is brown.

He forks whole, small potatoes
into his potato head.

There is also a bowl,
a jug,
a loaf perhaps.

It is dark,
probably an evening
and after work in the fields
there is nothing but the taste
of potato hot on his tongue
and soft in his teeth.

What he wants
is to eat the apples of the earth,
to become earth itself.

He must finish
before the stranger arrives.

With his eyes closed
he is in a solitary seat
in a solitary moment.

In another direction
a spring landscape has moved
to green and blossom
under the cream clouds
folded over a blue horizon.

A FLEMISH LANDSCAPE

This mid-March snow
surprised the low lands
with its soft shroud
thrown over dark green and bare trees.

The unseasonable deaths
of birds and insects.

Pelted by snow
the ditched backseat of a car
is draped with icy ermine,
where a buttery girl
and her hunter
could be enthroned.

A clutter of crows
lifts from the copse
into the blank canvas.

DAI GREATCOAT VISITS WATERLOO

From the top of the stiff lion's hill
the easterly cuts you to the bone
       on such a man-made moel,
coming from where the maps show Blucher
       and his Huns rushing in to save the day.

Wellesley held there
       a fine CO who'd cut his teeth in India
and the Peninsula against the Imperium,
mercenaries, no doubt, on all sides
together with the press'd and conscripted,
       all become Wealcyn.

Seems that Tommy, the good Huns and Orangemen
saw Boney turn heels on that long and bloody'd day
and slouch back to an island confine
       where, it is said,
the arse-nick'd wallpaper did for him.
A rum story.

Cluster'd bleak stone monuments *sans grace* –
Victor Hugo, General Gordon, Hanovarians, Belges.
It's in the nature of such stuff to make heroes of the brass
while infantry chaps, thousands of 'em,
go into the ground unsung,
       strip't of tunica and boots
and patted down with the flat of a spade.
Memento etiam Domine.
They prized out their teeth for false 'uns.

One feels that neck-tingle
and the pricking of a tear at Hougoumont Farm
where the stout grenadiers – Coldstreams and Jocks,
cursed themselves for hacking down doors
to fire their billy-brew the night before
       that would've been musket rests and firing cover-
but we held the gate against a hard, long day's assault
by Boney's Garde Imperial. They who fell in ranks
within the termini of the farm walls.

Now glimpsed through the grille of the tiny chapel
the feet of our Lord singed that day
are singed for ever.
                    Arglwydd – crucified black and grey.

A hundred years peace – until our own Show –
I suppose, was won at that Farm.

          Out on the fields the red line squared up,
bayonets knelt before muskets
               saw their cavalry repulsed
so the poor beasts piled up into bloody parapets.

No need for trenches,
               'cept to bury the fallen –
poor, stripped buggers forever etc.
               some corner of a Belgian field.
Uniforms and personals filched by the infernal followers.

Hand to mouth, hand to hand, the bad breath of the kill.
(Things hardened into the mechanical in our Show
with death dealt out distant, through gun sights)

One moment: old Wellie snapping shut his telescope,
then waving his hat to send our chaps after their rout,
standing high in his stirrups
                    on the bay Copenhagen
to survey the confusion.

Men ploughing the mud
               with their sweet faces.
In paradisium deducant te Angeli
For there had been no help on that open plain
save the embrace of the enemy.

MORNING ON THE MEUSE

The hotel begins to empty
and the suits are on the river bank
with their mobiles
looking for a signal.

The broad barges that work the river
push with, or shunt against, the flow
of the spring-swollen Meuse,
both green and brown through the day,
steady, full and wide, a river road
from the Ardennes that has cut past Verdun
and on to the North Sea.

Downstream there are herons,
cormorants, refineries, quarries,
the locks and traffic lights.

And here's *Genevieve*
her folding funnel and aerial mast,
a curtained cockpit and the captain's Merc
strapped to a ramp at the stern.

These barges are tankers, or open bunkers-
football pitches of gravel, heaped coal, sand,
bellied so low it seems a swell,
a passing bow-wave, would slop
over her side and swamp her.

Facing the Pont Albert
is a naked rider on his bare-backed horse.
Too formal to be a Frink – a king
clearly above other naked men,
high and secure against a sky
that shows the western weather
rolling in from France and England.

This is a river city
in a land defined by rivers
– the Meuse, the Marne, the Somme –
big water-hawsers holding the land in regions,
working rivers, arteries we bled for.

DARK NIGHT OF THE SOUL

for Ana Maria Pacheco

This is how it was –

Under the bluest of skies
on a mound between the city walls and the slow river
the Emperor's archers notch and draw their bows
taking aim at his body
strung, like his Lord, high on a tree.
He does not feel the piercings,
his eyes fixed on the above
that is out of the picture.

No one remembers after the arrows,
how they did no more than pierce and scar,
wounds that the love of Irene, a saint, could heal.
No, they finished him off later
with their clubs, beating him to a pulp,
for turning to the Faith.

This is how it is –

We can only imagine his face
under the black hood
if we choose to.
Bound to the stake by rope
and fallen to his knees, he flexes against the arrows.
Four men in leather coats surround him
and the people – men, women and babies, ourselves –
come across the scene as if by chance.

No one knows what he has done.
It could be anything, or nothing.
There is no State of Faith.
But this is the way things are,
this is how we may end.
Everything is larger than a life.

A face
The glacial white in rugged forms
Edges that blur
Edges that form flowered ridges
A red trough
The reclining nude
Is a corpse
The head of his son
His wife
His friends
All skulls
Pushing though
The angles of seeing
Face as landscape
Where the light catches
And forms shadows of depth
Paint thicker than skin
As if rendering them
This way
Made the passing less likely

Auerbach

WILLIAM BROWN'S *CIRCUS*

The bear
rears up to dance
decorated with light.
He cavorts, he struts
through the hearts, the love-spoons,
dances past a chequer board,
the cycling seals:
for this is the circus
of good and bad dreams.
There is no audience
save the two-legged horse,
the startled, small moon-bear,
the Loup-Garou with his teeth and claws,
a wolf riddled with guilt,
two impossibly red herrings,
and you, my friends, you.
Ladies and gentlemen
and now...
(applause, applause)

PRENDERGAST'S QUARRY

Bruised skies tumble over Eryri
drenching the land
under the god-governed, paper-torn clouds
until the colours run

through that squat stone chapel,
the spiky church spire,
near where the houses huddle
between stone walls at Deiniolen.

Rain slips blue light down slate slopes
and settles in the black cauldron of Penrhyn.
Weather and the water's clock
happens whether you paint it or not.

ABANDONED BARGE – COLIN JONES

Rising from the silt a beached axle-tree.
What is in the world, may also be a sign:
we see what we want there to be.

This mud-banked boat
at Lydney on the Severn
had a working life, turn and turn about,

coming to this point of rest.
Was worked by the weather
and the big tides' press:

the moon-pulled sea rising full
for the Vernal and Autumnal sluicing
of this river, turning everything over.

So you stopped that day
to look, and sketched this split hull –
the shaded mud, the lines of force,

hollowed spaces around the world's wide pole,
the warped keel and winged spars
risen like a spectre,

the carpenter's challenge,
the bare abstraction of the cross
you'd come to witness.

WORKING THE BEECH

For David Nash

It's the opening of a book,
a first encounter with that
rough-edged, sweet, sappy smell
as the wood smiles, splits
and grows into a new self. Look.

Two centuries and more in the growing
to this point of necessary felling:
eight-foot lengths, four foot span.
Chalk-marked and chain-sawed
along lines only he has seen,
the wood asserts itself
and begins to instruct the man.

The *Branch and Bole Column,*
a *Crack and Warp,* the *Split Frame,*
the *Tumbling Blocks,*
each piece stationed in a room.
So we shall witness
the drying, the variable split and turn
as wedge and sliver breathe out water.

From a working as messy as any birth
he's set you going in a new life:
fallen beech, angled and shaped,
the changes come more subtle than any of your seasons,
this curling and softening of colours
through your long and final autumn.

RICHARD LONG'S *BUZZARD*

From high soaring on thermals
The tame buzzard lays a flight path
Straight down through the paddock
To the bare oak:

This shallow trench line
Filled with Norfolk flint –
Shards, knuckles, yellow-white bones,
What remains of us.

MOORE

When his mother came back each night
from the laundry exhausted
he would rub liniment into her shoulders
until they eased.
This was the anatomy lesson of love,
the boy learning and exploring,
re-forming the first body.

Run your hand over the surface of her leg,
the solid, ridged bronze, his vision made large –
women as bones, bones under their gowns,
set high against the trees on the hill.
Another essay on the body,
the dynamics of something in bulk and at rest
until you love it back into life.

THE STONE COLLECTOR

Wedges of slate from Corris Uchaf and Bethesda,
Planted upright in our garden so the eye draws a line
Between them angled from trees and the hedge.

A pebble from Oric, Oregon where the cold Pacific roared
Has circles of quartz like surf
In a stone the colour of wet seals.

An old coffee jar holding Pembrokeshire pebbles
Filled with water,
To bring out their sheen and their colour.

The blue-green white-veined pebbles from Manorbier –
A favourite source where that wedge of sand
Pushes between Gerald's castle and the church where Piper drew.

A heavy lump of flint from Mametz,
Where the Welsh were cut down by the guns in the wood,
Is gas yellow, with glints from its murderous edges.

Paperweight on my desk,
A stone from Rhoose Point is limestone speckled
Like a constellation.

Remember the small prayer stones
On the headstones in the Jewish section
Of the Jacksonville graveyard in that goldrush town.

Three Welsh pebbles on the bookcase
By two Inuit soapstone figures –
A sea-bird, a man hunting seals.

From Jones Beach, New York, that flat, pure white stone
Picked up when we visited our son,
Fitting still my hand's grasp.

GOING WEST

Under a pewter sky
the air is rain-drenched.
The Atlantic has leaned in heavily
over Pembrokeshire and between
St. Clears and Llanddowror the Taf has laked
brown and grey over the green meadows.
February has over-filled the fields
and stocked the water levels for Spring.

All this is necessary and forgivable,
even the disappearance of Caldey Island
in the low cloud and rain, as I turn the Tenby corner,
for later that afternoon it comes back
green and clear in the last of the light.
This where we came west to the ocean;
this was landfall for the Irish saints coming east.
The waves spume tributes of silver over St Margaret's point.

TURNING

Stopping for salt-marsh lamb
from Eynons – *Purveyors of Fine Meats,*

on the Blue Boar bridge in the centre of St. Clears,
if you had not turned to double-check the car

that heron priesting the river
would have remained in the blue-grey shade

of overhanging trees, statuesque, dabbing
into the Cynin's shallow, pebbly flow,

an un-witnessed river-lord,
before turning and loping into the air

Laugharne-wards, spreading
his black, grey and white surplice against the sky.

AT GUMFRESTON CHURCH

That evening, after a hard, hot drive,
The dark lane's coolness of trees
Was like water walked into,
Calm and quiet – no traffic,
Deep shadows,
All the gulls out at sea.

Augustus and Gwen's father
Walked the two miles from Tenby
Every Sunday to play the organ here.
I search for his headstone and find no-one
But Ken Handicott the grocer
I worked for one school summer holiday
Forty years ago.

They leave the church door unlocked:
There is no congregation but the curious passing folk.
And inside is the simple spendour of stone font,
Low wooden roof, draped altar, Norman-built
On earlier significance – St. Teilo, St. Bridget.
The place shivers in the dusk
And moves into another night.

Here were the early missions, saints and sinners
Crossing the Irish Sea, moving east
With their crosses and swords.
Here was a quay, a village the river Ritec
Joined to the sea that led to the world.

And here, behind the church, before the woods
Where the Magdalens brought their lepers,
Still flow the three springs of purity
And healing, coming to us from a depth.
Water that plays the oldest music.

Without thinking
I take a handful
And with wet, cool fingers
Cross myself.

THE FOLLY

I wanted us to climb Paxton's Tower
but the cold January squall
kept you in the car at the bottom of the hill.
At least the mud path was still frozen firm
and now my view from the top of the stone stairs
is clear and wide – the Towy's flood plain
shining and more than half full.

All my life I'd glimpsed this folly
on our way east from Carmarthen.
Paxton promised the town
a new bridge over the river
but the voters would have none of him:
piqued, he built this oddity instead
and dedicated it to Nelson, our saviour.

In the growing dark of the afternoon
the rich cow pastures decline
from flooded silver to some baser stuff, lead.
What we knew, or thought we knew, is something other
than belief or faith and from this height
lacks certainty in the shifting light
and the alchemy of water.

LAST RIGHTS

Let it be done in the manner of Dr William Price:
then my ashes be given to the sea
off a boat visible from Tenby links
and bound for the island of Caldey.

I'm minded to emulate Peter's recent coffin –
wicker, with flowers and herbs of the season
woven roughly into the sides.

Though hymns are fine,
the balance should be in that space
between hope and scepticism and fears:
so let there be no more than one – *Calon Lan*;
and then Steely Dan's *Reeling in the Years* –
room enough for all to fix their thoughts.

Vaughan Williams' *Fantasia on a Theme by Thomas Tallis*,
or the second movement of his *Pastoral* symphony,
its plaintive Flanders trumpet for those who'd died,
sounding over the rolling green fields of England –
Berkshire, where the Curtises worked for centuries;
you decide.

And between those let there scratch out the Caedmon
wax recording of *Death Shall Have no Dominion*
in the sonorous tones of Dylan's contracted BBC.
Gulls cry at my ears
and waves break loud on the seashores.
Then choose three poems of my own.

At my going you may crack into smiles and spill tears
in equal measure:
let the rain in your face or the sun on your back
be that day's remembered pleasure.

FRAGILE TISSUE

i.m. Ceri Jones

Time to unwrap the painting –
its enigma: paper, tissue, string,
a Swansea childhood's premonitions,
and dawn's persistence each day
awakening the curve of bay.

The boy's half-slung-on morning coat:
his back to the terrace on the hill.
He turns away from that silver bay,
shining, flat and new, to face you.
The enigma of our fragile tissue.

There are no rocks, there was no siren,
no wineglasses break at this Swansea dawn.
There is no arrow, no target.
All a poet's lies: the cry of the guitar,
is nothing more than the way

a gull cries for itself, for
anyone who'll listen, or wants to dream
of white camellias from the south.
Lorca told you lies,
the poets always do.

Listen instead to Charlie Parker:
let Bird's be-bop alto shake up the melody,
cut through those tired songs you thought you knew:
he'll scrapple from the apple, though 'round midnight
the wistful mood deepens into melancholy.

Unwrap, unwrap the painting's
enigma – paper, tissue, string,
a Swansea childhood's premonitions,
and dawn's insistence that each day we sing,
awake the curve of the bay.

Leaving the terrace on the hill,
he turns away from the ugly town's lovely bay,
towards all his remaining years, to face you.
The green, half-worn coat covering him,
as boys do their tough and fragile tissue.

BARAFUNDLE BAY

i.m. John Tripp

It's late in the day
when I clamber down to the beach,
mid September, the arse end of summer.
Dexter
      &
Daisy
SEREN FREUD
written in the sand, letters five feet high.

A stiff Irish wind is playing in my ear
so I turn to the east and look beyond
the bobbing lobster boat,
the red sandstone cliffs of Stackpole,
to Manorbier's castle and white church tower.
Then the western edge of Caldey Island and beyond,
sinking like a black apple into the night,
Dylan's Gower always, John, always
out of reach for us.

The *summer's gone over the hill,* John,
and I'm no *rough weather guest.*
The sea curls back into itself.
The surfers and dog walkers have gone:
now I'm the only one.
I choose and pocket three pebbles – limestone
with veins of pink and white.

I take off my socks and shoes to paddle
at the edge of the retreating waves.
Clear, clean and cold, it wraps around my calves.
This feels like dying from the toes up.

John, you might have wished for such a salty end –
our friend Mike coming out of the sea in Normandy
was dead before he hit the sand.
But your heart gave out, bruised and sour,

on your old man's settee in the Whitchurch bungalow,
the early hours tv showing a blizzard of nothing.

The last fishing boat turns away
from its implausibly orange lobster buoy.
One by one I throw my pebbles at the sea.
Barafundle – *the Atlantic lash*, as you said,
will turn *its storm eye on all frivollers* such as we –
Dexter & Daisy and Seren, the sand-scratched names,
John, the living and the dead.

THE PLOT

Turning off the Ridgeway to the Manorbier road
you linger in second after that slow bend
to take in again the stunning view of Caldey –
beach, lighthouse, monastery – set in the bluest sea,
just before dropping down the corkscrew lane between
high-banked hedges snow-drifted with constellations
of sweet and musty Queen Anne's lace,
the garlic's sour-sweet flowers like distant stars,
and passing over the railway line
to the chapel where your mother
has reserved her plot, the most prudent of things
in this country where the light and the summer sings.

THE ALVIS HARE

The hare you've set me to chase
comes up on *Google* as a bonnet creature,
a car mascot, Mum, as you'd thought;
off a pre-war low-slung Alvis roadster,
the one you saw last Sunday afternoon
in The Battle of Britain,
when Michael Caine drives to his Spitfire base.

It can't have been from that heavy, long, black,
Mulliner limo we drove for a few months in the late '50s,
distinguished among the dozens of Austins and Ford Pops
that passed through our lives and carried us
on Dad's trips to family in Berkshire, to the Williams in Bangor,
our pilgrimages to the obscure and famous –
flooded Lynmouth, up the Air Balloon, there and sometimes back.

In later years this hare was perched alongside
Veteran Motorist and Caravan Club badges, an AA shield,
under the front grilles on his bumper bar.
Alert, up on hind legs, the chrome hare
has now a dulled glow from the fumes and spray,
the grit of journeys only you and I remember
and compose, the cars and the man who died.

THE TRENCHES AT GILTAR

We make way into the westerly
behind a golf umbrella, pressed
against the flow of weather,
an April flurry of rattling showers,
up the headland path into the last of the light.

The map of Giltar promised trenches
where the Tommies practised drill and assault.
Those shallows twisting through tight cliff grasses
must have been a warm, spring bed
in another world before Mametz and Arras.

St Margaret's Island and Caldey are calf and whale,
greys and greens set in sparkling water.
The sea tonight is deepest aquamarine,
the tide baring its teeth in the narrow sound.
At our backs, the evening's lights coming on in Penally.

This handful of softened foxholes,
freshly turned earth;
a sheep curl out of the weather
where a man might lie and look up
for a pattern of clouds or stars.

            There's a lull
between the lobbing of Mills bomb-stones –
the itch of stiff khaki, his oily fingers
tracing the ridges of the Lee Enfield.

And then

            the barked commands,
the cold fixing of bayonets.

Those moments when the sky
            is a sheet folded
down to the level sea,

            the quiet movement
of a symphony.

AN EVENING WALK TO THE SEA

I walk right into the view, in a determined line,
through the gate, over the first field to the horizon trees,
those three (are they hawthorns?) prominent against the sky.
Take aim at them, as surely as a bird's flight to the sea.

Tramping up to that tree-line to discover
undistinguished, some mayflower merged into an everyday hedge;
and the view now of another field, and yet another,
the sea not as near, or real as I'd imagined it to be.

And the houses, the M.O.D. ordnance at Skrinkle too close
                for comfort.
But following the line of the hedge as it falls towards Carmarthenshire
I'm offered that priceless view of Caldey and beyond, quite clear,
Burry Port and the Worm's Head on the Gower.

Walk until the corner is gated and blocked by a pill-box,
brick-built, topped with concrete, two-, three-manned;
their bevelled machine-gun slots covering the invasion,
traversing from the Pembroke road to Lydstep Caverns.

Its shrapnel-angled entrance to the north, inland;
dirty wool, cattle stubble on the barbed wire;
a dry but bare earth-trodden floor –
all now buttressed into peacetime hedges.

The summer of '44, last watch: a man stretched across
the concrete roof, loosed tunic, smoking, cradling his Bren,
watching the herd amble back from milking, lorries gathering at
                Skrinkle.
He jumps down, slams shut the door. A train to Hampshire. Caen.
        Berlin.

YOSEMITE

Clouds Cristo-wrap El Capitan
and erase the top of the Falls;
then an afternoon of heavy rain.
After the Oregon Trail Monologue
– prairie mud, smallpox, the grubby prospectors –
we go out into a pitch night
that the rain has washed clear
and on up through the huge pines meet
a sky that comes down to greet us
with its diamond stars, clustered and close,
silver, shining and without number,
as if for the first time. As if,
out on that vast prairie seeking a new life,
we saw what we were in the middle of.

SIRENS

Stopping off 101 to check the map
something pulls us over the dune ridge
to the wild blue of the Pacific at Oric.
Then down the boardwalk across the grit,
past the bleached sculpture of the driftwood trees,
to the sand with its crab claws,
stripped-white bony twigs.

Down to the roaring sea from which rise
the ponderous pelicans with their great, hinged beaks
gliding over the silver-grey roll of the seals
playing at the surf-break to fish the shore.
As we enter the blue cold of the sea,
the gravel gives way and the icy undertow
grips our ankles like hands.

THE LIGHT

for James Turrell

This light is vintage –
Grown three and a half billion years
To be tasted like a fine wine
In the decanter of Roden Crater.

You must close out the arid horizon,
Climb above Arizona
Into the bare volcano cup of this place,
A cathedral of ash and air,
Where you may stand or lie
Prepared to receive the sky
As a pure, infinite, un-peopled realm.
The stars form their endless patterns
And the depth of field is the quiet sublime.
That's when the sky moves backwards
And shows the earth's turning.

When his grandmother took the small boy
Into the Friends House
They simply sat. Not a word.
They sat for a long time and he asked why.
Why, to greet the light, she said,
And pointed to the sky.

THE FAMINE MUSEUM

For Ed Boyne
who could not go in

That summer of 'forty-six
Again the flies fed on the blighted people.
With the potatoes rotting in the baskets
And nothing to eat or plant
Whispered sedition rose to a shout
Against the landed and their fat managers.
Oakboys and Rightboys and Lady Rocks
Wore their wives' shawls and in the hedgerow scailps
Swore to fight and die for each other.

When Major Mahon was shot
At the Doorty bridge on the Roscommon road
The army rigged a trial and hanged Patrick Hasty.
They filled old ships with the evicted poor
And sailed them out to Canada,
A middle passage that grew
More skeletons, typhus and dysentery.
At Grosse Isle, Quebec, the quarantine men
Used boat-hooks to pull out the dead.

We learn these things, today at Strokestown Park,
In Mahon's fine house,
Where the servants entered and left by tunnels
To spare offence, out of sight and mind,
And the melon house was heated,
So grapes and peaches and chrysanthemums
Bloomed all the year round.

We walk back out into meadows of sun
Where the sheep cling to the oak's shade,
The stream flows clear and fast and see
Just there, a fine trout – a full pound, I'd guess –
Breaks out of the emerald weeds
And muscles upstream.

THE FINAL SHIFT

Called to the foreman's office
at fifteen minutes to five.
You've done your time Stephens,
fifty years. Here's your packet.
Off you go, man, you go early today.
The rope loosed, weight lifted, direction unclear.

He walked to the foundry gates and looked out.
A summer breeze, poppies in the ditch,
elderflower creaming the line of the hedge,
the sky blue, with light, high clouds.
The coal train's whistle coming down the valley,
Then the afternoon hooters.

He pulled his cap on against the sun
and undid his waistcoat buttons one by one.

JOHN PETTS AT THE FALLS

The heavy rain on his light head
all that walk up through the woods
filled with blossom and the presence
of grey ponies.

He took a quiet while
under the long cascade of Aber Falls
before shouting out loud –
Why should I sigh, Lord,
as silver hairs stream down the brow?
– for the sheer, sheer silver of a thousand strings
was descending and seething till he was won
and one with the water, the blossom, the ponies.

A cold tingling as the water dried on his face
and there in the speckled light of the green trees
was a memory of the soldiers he'd ministered
on the Rhine and in Palestine –
etching their veins with his morphine needle,
then dipping his fingers in their blood
to mark the brows of the dying
with an *M* and the time of their release.

He drove further north that day
to visit Kyffin Williams on Ynys Mon
between the two Menai bridges,
who was planting lemon-balsam
in the verges of his lane,
so that, at his coming and going,
his boots and tyres would throw
their sweetness into the air.

CROSSING OVER

Three days out from England,
The summer-calm Atlantic lulled us with sun
And the last U-boats lay deep like drowsy fish
Waiting for the music of pistons.
Cloudless and hot, so we let the POWs take the air
And a stretch on the after-deck, hundreds of them
In murmuring huddles, bleary and pacing those confines.

Above them, a row of American aircrew headed home,
Perched on the rail facing the bows, away
From the grey dregs of that beaten army.
Those sheepskin and leather flying jackets
We so envied, worn loose now in the heat.
They flexed their arms like boxers lifting weights,
Punching each other in play.

And when those strong young men
With their war-tightened faces
Turned to go to the mess, we saw why
They'd broadened their backs above the Germans.
Every man's jacket proclaimed *Berlin Dresden Cologne*
Each raid commemorated with a painted nose-down bomb –
Six, eight, eleven missions through the shrapnel.

As we docked at our final berth those fliers
Were soused in bourbon and grew louder,
As men come through it all, against the odds,
Will shout their lives out to the sky,
Slapping backs, jitterbugging man with man,
Then blowing up their last French letters
To launch them as love zepplins towards Manhattan.

TAKING YOUR FOOD

The beginning of the end of the war –
Patton's Third Army fought into Brittany
and the Wehrmacht crumbled apart,
when you were five.
                    A child
in uniform – fourteen, fifteen maybe –
stumbled into the barn, crazy with hunger,
threw his rifle down, sending a bullet into the wall.
He stretched into the pickling tub
to grab a piece of the belly pork
and you all watched him eat it raw.

In Algiers your platoon
trawled the Casbah for the FLN bomber –
doors kicked open, screams, tables overturned,
the warm, couscous and peppers slippery underfoot.
But what made you National Service boys want to heave
was the reek of a half-skinned goat left hanging from a rafter.
After Algeria you had to leave.

Learning to wait tables at The Paradise Hotel.
"Les *entrées* – pourquoi?"
In your cigarette breaks out on the stoop
you'd look across the Susquehanna
to the Catskills – endless trees, numberless greens –
America going on for ever.

Then the move into Queens as Maitre D'
– you had the accent, knew the score.
The elegant Gregory Peck.
Kissinger, a nervy eater.
Jackie O, quiet, swan-like.
And Old Blue Eyes –
with the most beautiful chicks you've ever seen,
well connected, like he owned the place,
always going out back to the kitchen,

to thank everyone. Big tipper,
scattering bucks like confetti.
That was style. There was a guy
knew how to dine.

THE MORNING ROUND

I see the rooks are building high
in the wood behind the club,
and you say that means a decent spring.
They fly with beaks full of nesting stuff,
though today a stern westerly
is waltzing them across the sky.
So, playing's tough – our drives
are bent, the putts won't drop.

We talk in sound-bites between the squalls.
If you can't murder me today.
She had me up at three.
You're not getting any nights.
She's on the morphine now,
the end's in sight.

If we were proper friends,
or I were stronger, I'd linger
for a coffee, offer help:
Anything we can do.
Just ask. Anything.
Though I sense that's not the thing for you –
dry humour, going sour is your way.

The westerly brings in steady rain
and the umbrellas go up.
Jaw, jaw. Come on,
just play the shot,
is what you say.

LATE FALL

This year the later Fall,
a surprising November,
and each round takes longer
– the walk from green to tee,
the crossing of the fairways,
the rain-flattened rough –

for each fallen maple leaf,
damp-curled, face down,
needs to be turned over, spread
so that it shines – brown
and bronze, black and grey,
orange and red.

TUSCANY POSTCARDS FOR JOAN

i.m. Joan Abse

I

From the summit of the Boboli Gardens
the view is pure Tuscany postcards –
soft hills that roll endlessly
with houses and churches set between
olives and cypresses.
                    At the foot
of this sheer wall, closer houses holding their ordinary lives –
the edge of a bed, a small television.
In a clutch of olives and apricots
an abandoned Land Rover is filled with sticks,
dry grasses covering its tyres.

2

In the Porcelain Museum – Worcester,
Vienna, Vincennes, Sévres –
coldly displayed in great glass cases:
grand palaces, Chinoiserie, Egyptian dogs and geometry;
death-cheating flower arrangements in paint.

                    In the sunlit entrance,
there's a cat stretched out on the carpet
you'd have bent to stroke, Joan.

3

A little boy is wrapt
with his head stuck through the curved railings.
He is fascinated by the Oceanus, the tubs of lemon trees,
the fish and the circuit of ducks around the Isolotto.

His mother looks back with her arm outstretched.
but says nothing.
                            She leaves him
in the moment.

What of this will he remember?

4

Ice Cold in Florence.
We drink chilled beers,
pick at the bowls of agnoli marinelli
and read the labels of the malt and bourbon.

One side of the Piazza is San Felicita
where a priest was saying mass though a microphone
to six or eight of the faithful –
the other, Casa Gaudi where Robert
and Elizabeth Barrett settled their love.
And wrote and loved and wrote.

As you enter San Felicita
the doors' brief light offers Filippino Lippi's
S. Rocco, S. Anthony and S. Catherine.
The supporting narrative has Catherine pressed between
two bladed wheels, like some accident waiting to happen,
that in another scene has already taken her
from life into eternity.

Though the desperate and the dull
take the Bible and the Quaran
to be no more than the literal,
the great artists and surely, Joan, your Ruskin
knew that imagery was the distillation
of our living: pictures to guide us
through the wondrous mess.

5

On the Ponte Santa Trinite,
couples catch with their cameras
the view and each other:
posed on the east parapet against the backdrop
of the Arno and the Ponte Vecchio,
moments snatched between the traffic –
Their day in Florence fixed in the screen.

6

Barga's Duomo is empty,
so I climb into the Bigarelli pulpit, its legs supported by lions.

There's the life of Christ in relief –
stars, palms, whips, nails.

And scored and felt-tipped graffiti
Guido/Sebastian 1983
on the opened book carved into the stone ledge.

The portal doors frame Monte di Croce –
the coming weather like a scarf wrapped around its neck.

Barga has a thousand-year-old carving in wood behind the altar
that looks like a faux naïf work of our century –

S. Christopher with the Child perched on his shoulder,
held high and dry above the troubles of the world.

On the far bank Christopher set down his burden –
the Christ Child.
And then his staff

which grew and bore dates in that ground
and here, olives.

7

The green lizard with its yellow and black speckles
has shared his terrace with us all the day.
Those hot, hazy views down to Lucca,
the mewing buzzards high above
and around us the inky, blue-black bees
sinking themselves in the flower heads.

This evening's peach and plum sky
holds a broken porcelain moon over the hill.

Joni and K.D. Lang singing through the dark:
                    Just like Jericho,
the walls come tumbling down.

One of those evenings when the world almost falls into place.

8

The Trattoria Tre Torri
at Portovenere still serves an insalata di mare
with the sweetest, tiny fish and calamari –
just as in '96, Joan, when we came to celebrate Shelley
and commemorate his daft death.

The crazy fool was taken by a sudden storm
in the Golfo dei Poeti, a mill pond even bent Byron
had swum easily with his club foot trailing like an anchor.

At the foot of the Chiesi S. Pietro today
we had a squall of warm rain; and afterwards
looking down into the Byron Grotto saw
a bearded man unloose his heavy hair and take to the water.

In that green bay he turned and floated like the poet,
or some figure of Christ held like an insect in amber.

Joan, you would have thought of tempera, lapis lazuli,
an illumination of the text,
and smiled as he looked up at us.

THAT *MUSIC LOVER'S LITERARY COMPANION*

Dannie, your book with Joan
of musical quotes and poems
arrives this morning from a dealer on Amazon
and out drops a hedgehog-shaped green notelet:

*Mr Lewis, I thought you might
not speak to me if I said no!*
  Alison
(I'll bring the ticket for the concert on Thursday)

And inscribed at the end of August, ninety-two
on the flyleaf it says:

   To Mr Lewis
   Thank you!
   Love
   Alison Outhwaite

Mr Lewis and his grateful, Oxford-bound girl:
what symphony, prelude, soloist, what choir sang for them?
What brush of fingers, sharing the programme?
And later, at home in bed, skimming the *Companion*,
he'd have read that night:

The plush curtains opening...

   Woke into voice each silent string.

 What melodious nonsense...

   ...the unclouded concerto...

...the melodies weep and smile...

 O delight cascading the weirs of the spine...

Now I have him closing the book and setting the alarm;
he plumps the pillow, turns off the reading light;
then he kisses his wife goodnight.

FROM THE GARDEN

Pearls on the clothes line
after rain.

Not enough blue in the sky
to stitch a sailor's suit;

but there's the chemical blue of the rat bane
in the plastic tray I've left on the path
for the squirrels rioting in our loft.

*

Your greenhouse has forced such life
from the tired, old, barbed cactus
that we bring it into our living room:

bright orange splashes
with creamy white stamen

against the Ceri Richards
Lion Hunt after Delacroix.

*

My spade turns over a stone
shaped like a sabre-tooth fossil,
a digging tool from ages before

lacking only its shaft, some purpose say,
for the wooden handle's gone to earth,
the fashioning hand to clay.

SLOW WORM

After the hottest of April days,
in the late, slanting sun,
there's a bronzed arabesque

lying on the coping stone
of your herb-border wall – the bright
gold torc of a Silerian queen

pulled up into the light –
that's slid back between the cool bricks,
just now as I looked away.

And because you are not here
I must fashion these words
into a shape you'd wear.

Acknowledgements

Ambit, The David Jones Journal, Descant, Magma, New Welsh Review, Seam, South, Planet, Poetry London, Poetry Wales, Quattrocento, Roundyhouse, Skald, Van Gogh's Ear.

Light Unlocked: Christmas Card Poems (Enitharmon), *Considering Cassandra: Poems and a Story* (Gwasg Carreg Gwalch), *Wading Through Deep Water* (Coychurch Press); *Only Connect* (Cinammon Press). 'Late Fall' was a Valleys Lines Train poem. 'A Noble Going' was short-listed for the Strokestown Poetry Competition. "'Mapping the World' was BBC Radio Wales National Poetry Day choice.

'Cathédrale engloutie' was included in *The Guardian* Villanelle website workshop by Tony Curtis in 2006.